Cities through Time

Daily Life in
Ancient and Modern

by Sarah Hoban

illustrations by Bob Moulder

RP

Runestone Press/Minneapolis
A division of Lerner Publishing Group

The *Cities through Time* series is produced by Runestone Press, a division of Lerner Publishing Group, in cooperation with Greenleaf Publishing, Inc., Geneva, Illinois.

Cover design by Michael Tacheny
Text design by Melanie Lawson, Jean DeVaty, and Rebecca JonMichaels

Runestone Press
A division of Lerner Publishing Group
241 First Avenue North
Minneapolis, Minnesota 55401 U.S.A

Website address: www.lernerbooks.com

Library of Congress Cataloging-in-Publication Data

Hoban, Sarah.
    Daily life in ancient and modern Paris / Sarah Hoban; illustrated by Bob Moulder.
        p.   cm. — (Cities through time)
    Includes index.
    Summary: Explores daily life in Paris, from the time of its early settlement in the seventh century B.C. through the Middle Ages up to two world wars and after.
    ISBN 0-8225-3222-0 (lib. bdg. : alk. paper)
    1. Paris (France)—Social life and customs—Juvenile literature. [1. Paris (France)] I. Title. II. Series.
    DC715.H53   2001
    944'.361—dc21   99-042056

Manufactured in the United States of America
1 2 3 4 5 6 – JR – 06 05 04 03 02 01

Contents

NORTH
ATLANTIC
OCEAN

English Channel

Modern-day border

N

Paris

Seine

FRANCE

MEDITERRANEAN SEA

Introduction

Paris, the capital of France, sits at the heart of the Île-de-France, a broad basin of land. Five rivers, the Seine, Oise, Marne, Ourcq, and Aisne, ring the fertile lands of the basin. Paris, the City of Light, is home to 2.2 million people. Its origins go back to the third century B.C., when a small group of people first settled on the Île de la Cité, a small island in the Seine River.

Throughout history, Parisians have used the river as a trade route and water source. These days the Seine is a scenic ribbon running through town, spanned by beautiful bridges.

The city is famous as a place of charm and as a center of European culture. Paris has inspired artists, writers, and musicians. Parisian philosophers and scholars have devised new ways of looking at the world. All across the globe, the name Paris conjures up thoughts of delicious food, beautiful fashions, and historic landmarks.

The city's charming streets have been the scene of riots, revolutions, sieges, and hardship. The people of Paris have battled foreign invaders as well as their neighbors. Parisians have suffered through famine, plagues, and poverty. They have seen parts of their city destroyed and then rebuilt. Along the way, the people of Paris have forged a beautiful city renowned throughout the world.

The Eiffel Tower *(left)* is the stunning emblem of Paris. The towers of Notre Dame Cathedral *(far left)* rise above the Île de la Cité.

Thick expanses of swamp protected the city from invasion.

Île de la Cité

The Parisii

In the seventh century B.C., the marshes, plains, and forests of the Île-de-France attracted Celtic Iron-Age settlers to the limestone hills near the Seine. About 400 years later, some moved to the Île de la Cité, where they built a village. They became known as the Parisii, or "boat people." They built long wooden houses and made their livings as fishers and traders on the Seine.

At that time, the Seine was a wide river with great stretches of marshland on either bank. The Parisii built wooden bridges linking the island to both riverbanks.

The island offered the Parisii protection from enemies, who would have to wade through the river to attack. The Parisii had reason to worry about invaders. Soldiers from the Roman Empire, led by the future

The Parisii charged tolls for using their bridges.

Fortifications controlled the passage of boats up and down the river.

Seine River

emperor Julius Caesar, were swiftly conquering Gaul (modern-day France). In 53 B.C., the Romans built a settlement on the Île de la Cité, which they named Lutetia Parisiorum.

The leaders of the conquered Celtic groups were supposed to become members of the Assembly of Gaul. When some leaders refused to attend in 52 B.C., the Romans moved the Assembly's meeting place to Lutetia. Celtic men and women across Gaul rebelled against the Romans. The Celts seized control of the Île de la Cité. When the large Roman army approached, the Parisii realized that they couldn't defend the island.

The Celts burned Lutetia and the city's many wooden bridges. Despite the Celtic destruction of Lutetia, the Romans soon won back control of Gaul.

Lutetia Parisiorum

The Romans rebuilt Lutetia, which soon grew into a main Roman settlement in northern Gaul. People in Lutetia traded jewelry, gold, and cloth across Gaul and the rest of Roman Europe. Lutetia also became a center of shipbuilding. By A.D. 200, the town had spread beyond the Île de la Cité to both sides of the river. A large cemetery and a temple sat on the river's Right Bank, north of the river. Most of the settlement centered on the island and the Left Bank (on the river's south side) and was encircled by a wall.

The builders modeled the new city on Rome. They laid out the streets in a geometric pattern and erected Roman-style stone buildings. Private homes

Amphitheater

Roman temple

Forum

Curia (town hall)

shared streets with commercial and public buildings, such as the forum (a market and meeting place), the basilica (a courthouse), and the curia (the town hall). The Parisii adopted Roman ways. They began speaking a dialect of Latin, the language of Rome, and intermarried with Roman newcomers.

The people of Lutetia lived a comfortable life. In winter they warmed themselves near charcoal-burning stoves. Ox-drawn carts carried people around the town. A 10-mile-long aqueduct brought fresh water from south of the city. Fancy public bathhouses were free on certain days, and fountains bubbled in public squares. A large amphitheater could hold fifteen thousand people, even though only about eight thousand people lived in Lutetia. In the amphitheater, eager spectators watched the slaughter of people belonging to a new religion, Christianity.

Paris Becomes Christian

The Romans were shocked by the Celts' religion, which included human sacrifice. Roman priests sacrificed animals instead of people. Over time, most people of Lutetia began to follow Roman religious practices. The Romans built temples to Mercury, the god of commerce and travel, and to the chief Roman god, Jupiter.

In A.D. 212, Lutetia was renamed Paris. About the same time, Parisians began to embrace Christianity. At first, these new Christians were killed or forced into hiding by Roman leaders, who saw the new religion as a threat. Even so, Parisians continued to convert. Then in 312, the Roman emperor Constantine I converted, making Christianity an official religion of the Roman Empire.

The fourth and fifth centuries were dangerous times for the Parisians. Germanic invaders from the east attacked Gaul, and in A.D. 422 they spared Paris only at the last minute. The city's population swelled with people from the countryside, who hoped for protection inside the city walls. But soon after, the city succumbed to invasion when the Germanic Franks attacked and conquered Paris. By 476 the Roman Empire was crumbling, and in 508 Paris became the seat of the Frankish Empire, which would give its name to France.

The Middle Ages (A.D. 500–1500) had begun. Life for most Parisians continued as it had under the Roman Empire. Yet some changes occurred. In 635 the Frankish ruler Dagobert established a trade and entertainment festival at the Church of Saint-Denis, on the edge of Paris. The annual festival drew merchants and travelers from across France and the world. In fact, sometimes so many people packed into churches to see holy relics during the festival that people were crushed to death.

Jugglers, beggars, thrill seekers, and pilgrims (religious travelers) headed to the annual festival at the Church of Saint-Denis.

10

The Church of Saint-Denis

The Headless Saint

A bishop named Denis worked to convert the citizens of Lutetia in the 200s. He founded many churches and converted many people to Christianity. The Roman authorities saw Denis as a threat and beheaded him.

The legend of Saint Denis claims that after he was killed, his still-living body picked up its own head, washed it in a stream, and walked five miles before dying. An abbey called Saint-Denis was built on the site of his grave. Over time, it became a beautiful cathedral where pilgrims paid homage to the saint.

The Vikings attacked the Île de la Cité's north bridge tower with arrows, stones, and battering rams. They also catapulted fireballs and launched blazing boats at wooden bridges and towers. In return, the Parisians poured boiling oil and molten tar onto the Vikings.

Paris's north bridge tower

Vikings on the Seine

Scandinavian invaders called Vikings were plundering much of Europe, including France, in the ninth century. Between A.D. 845 and 885, the Vikings sailed their longboats down the Seine to attack Paris six times. They looted the rich Parisian churches and monasteries, killing the people inside.

The Frankish emperor, Charles the Fat, did little to defend the city. Citizens appealed to the nobleman Odo, Count of Paris, for protection. By 885 the Parisians had crowded to the Île de la Cité for safety. Workers had rebuilt the ancient Roman wall and had constructed high wooden watchtowers, where guards watched both bridges. When Siegfried, a Viking leader, led a fleet of seven hundred boats down the river, he ordered the Parisians to remove a bridge so that his ships could pass. The Parisians refused, so the Vikings laid siege.

Although the people of Paris suffered from famine and cold weather, they refused to give up.

Count Odo begged Charles the Fat to help the city. Charles offered the Vikings a deal: If Siegfried would back down, Charles agreed to grant the Vikings passage along the Seine to the French region of Burgundy.

The Vikings agreed, but the deal infuriated the Parisians, who refused to let the ships pass. The Vikings were forced to detour, to put their ships on rollers, and to drag them overland around the city of Paris.

The people of Paris were disgusted with Charles the Fat. As a result, the Île-de-France broke away from the Frankish Empire, establishing the country of France. In A.D. 987, a Parisian descendent of Count Odo named Hugh Capet was elected king of the new nation.

Parisian guilds were active in different areas of the city. In the Grand Châtelet district, street names like La Grande Boucherie (the butcher shop) and Pied de Boeuf (ox foot) signaled what shoppers would find there. Scribes, illuminators, and stalls that sold parchment were housed in the Latin Quarter. Goldsmiths and money changers had their shops on the Grand Pont, the main bridge leading to the Île de la Cité.

These fifteenth-century French manuscript illustrations show customers and merchants bartering in the marketplace (top), tailors sewing clothes (right), and construction workers building a road on the city outskirts (opposite).

Paris at Work

Many different social groups lived together in medieval Paris. Vassals were workers who served landowning nobles or religious organizations. Under the feudal system, vassals gave military service, labor, or goods in exchange for protection and a place to farm or rent. Scholars and students lived in the city's Latin Quarter. Peasants brought farm goods to sell at Paris's vast open-air markets. Many Parisians were members of the bourgeoisie—free people who worked in trades. Some became extremely wealthy and powerful, but others barely scraped by.

In Paris and across medieval Europe, tradespeople, artisans, workers, and merchants banded into guilds. The organizations set the standards for each trade, regulated wages, and tried to keep working hours reasonable. Butchers, barbers, tailors, cobblers, knife makers, fishmongers, lace makers, and even thieves were members of guilds.

Although a few guilds (such as the lace makers) admitted only women, most guilds accepted only men. However, if a woman's husband died, some guilds allowed the widow to take over the family business. The road to becoming a guild member—a master—was a long one. Boys and girls were apprenticed between the ages of four and twelve and lived with the family of a master. Masters could beat, starve, overwork, or sell their apprentices. But many masters treated their apprentices kindly and taught them valuable skills.

Over the five to ten years of apprenticeship, the master taught the apprentice how to do the work and how to run a business. The apprentice then might become a journeyman, who traveled around practicing the trade. To become a master, the journeyman had to pass a difficult test and sometimes pay a large fee. Thus, some people never reached the honored position of master.

Barber

Traveling entertainers amused
shoppers and passersby.

Baker

River Life

Two main bridges, the Grand Pont (large bridge) and the Petit Pont (little bridge), connected the Île de la Cité with the rest of the city. More bridges linked the banks as the city grew. Even though bridges collapsed, burned, washed away in floods, or were smashed by ice, Parisians treated them as regular city streets.

Houses and shops lined the bridges. Parisians strolled across them on the way to sell or buy produce and animals at market. Beggars crouched in doorways. Street vendors sold everything from bread to pet birds to old shoes. Apothecaries (early pharmacists) prepared medicines in a number of shops on the Petit Pont, while barbers—including some women

Members of the watermen's guild regulated river traffic on the Seine. It was a powerful group, and in 1260 King Louis IX appointed leaders of the guild to administer the township of Paris. In modern times, the city's coat of arms bears the guild's symbol and the motto *Fluctuat nec mergitur*, meaning, "She is buffeted by the waves but does not sink."

Apothecary

barbers—shaved and groomed customers in their own shops. Bakers crying, "Warm patties, really hot! Warm pastries, scorching hot!" peddled hot meat patties made of chicken, pork, or eel and sweet pastries filled with custard or cheese. Traveling entertainers sang, played instruments, and commanded animals to do tricks.

Below the bridges rolled the Seine. Boats docked at piers that lined the banks. Merchants unloaded boats filled with produce and wine for the markets. In other boats, fishers trolled for carp and pike. From the banks of the river, citizens set out for a swim. But people also dumped garbage and sewage into the river, polluting the water.

Building Notre Dame

The Middle Ages in Paris were a time of building. A cathedral called Notre Dame de Paris was one of the grandest medieval structures ever built. It took almost 200 years to complete after Pope Alexander III laid the cornerstone in 1163. The plot of land on the Île de la Cité where Notre Dame was built had been used for religious practice as far back as Roman times, when it had housed a temple to the Roman god Jupiter.

Most of the stone for the cathedral and for other building projects came from quarries in the countryside surrounding Paris. To reduce the weight of the stone to be transported, workers cut the stone into rough shapes at the quarry. Workers then loaded the cut stone onto oxcarts or barges for the trip to the city.

Thousands of guild members worked to build Notre Dame. Stonemasons took the roughly shaped stone blocks and refined them, carving elaborate designs and decorations. Construction workers then heaved the massive stone pieces into place, using wooden scaffolding and ramps built by skilled carpenters. Ironsmiths forged and sharpened tools and made the heavy chains that laborers used to haul and lift the stone. Master stonemasons sculpted more than 1,200 statues to adorn the exterior, and glass workers created enormous, richly hued and intricately designed stained-glass windows.

The cathedral—completed in 1345—was a center of Parisian life. Pilgrims from the countryside traveled there to worship. Homeless beggars slept in the church and on its steps. Prisoners asked for sanctuary within its walls. Kings and princes prayed there for safety as they set out for battle and gave thanks if they returned safely home.

The square in front of the cathedral became an open-air stage where guild members performed religious plays. Guilds dramatized Bible stories and stories from the lives of saints in front of awestruck audiences. The plays featured large casts of guild members, who used their skills to create elaborate sets and special effects. Because of this tradition, the area became known as the Place du Parvis, which means "Place of Paradise."

Embedded in the pavement in the Place du Parvis is Point Zéro, a brass compass point that serves as the center point for measuring distances throughout France.

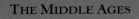

The great cathedral of Paris, Notre Dame, completed in A.D. 1345, soon became a haven for religious pilgrims, beggars, and royalty alike. It was the setting for Victor Hugo's famous novel *The Hunchback of Notre Dame*.

The student walking on the banks of the Seine in the evening ought not to indulge in sports but rather think about his lesson and repeat it.
—Robert de Sorbon, founder of the Sorbonne

A Seat of Learning

Up until the early thirteenth century, teaching in Paris took place in monasteries or at schools run by cathedrals. But around 1200, groups of scholars formed loose associations to devise rules for licensing teachers.

The scholars lived and taught in squalid rooms that they rented on the Left Bank of the Seine. But some patrons founded houses, called colleges, where a few teachers could live and teach. One college, the Sorbonne, became world famous and was known as the Académie Universitaire de Paris.

As more students came from all over Europe to study in Paris, patrons founded more colleges. The schools clustered in the Latin Quarter on the Left Bank.

Students could enter the university at age sixteen and were usually supposed to study for about ten years. They studied theology, canon (religious) law, the arts, and medicine. The teachers and students spoke in Latin, which made it easy for scholars across Europe to converse.

Parisians living near the universities didn't think much of the students. The students worked hard at their studies, but some pulled pranks or stole books and tools from merchants. In wine shops, brawls often broke out between students and other people.

A dangerous riot broke out in 1278 when a local abbey put up a few buildings along a path that students used to get to playing fields near the Seine. The students tore down the buildings. Monks from the abbey, along with their vassals, attacked the students. During the fight, two students were killed. Others were thrown into the abbey dungeon. But in spite of the rowdy students, by 1400 Paris was a center of learning for all of France and for Europe, with a total of about forty colleges. Famous medieval scholars who studied in Paris included Peter Abelard, Thomas Aquinas, and Roger Bacon.

(Above) A fourteenth-century seal from the Académie Universitaire de Paris. (Left) Louis IX, king of France from 1226 to 1270 and leader of the Seventh Crusade, studies with his tutor.

Care for the Sick

All across Paris, people threw their garbage into the streets to rot. Open sewers gave off an awful stench. Some people carried nosegays of sweet-smelling flowers to cover the odors. Most roads were dirt trails, so rain flooded them or turned them into thick mud. Rainstorms sometimes forced people to make bridges by laying planks across the streets. Houses lined winding streets so narrow that sunlight never reached the ground. The population of beggars was enormous. They slept in the streets and in churches. The city was cramped and crowded, conditions that made it easy for disease to spread.

But when the poor of Paris got sick, they did have a clean and safe place to stay. The Hôtel-Dieu, or God's Hostel, was founded in the 600s by Landry, the bishop of Paris, as a free hospital for the poor. The large hospital, located on the Seine near Notre Dame, accepted patients of any age, sex, or nationality. In time it became a refuge for the sick and the old from the streets of the city.

Patients at the Hôtel-Dieu found clean wards and fresh water that was pumped in from the river and heated—but dumped back in the river after it was used. Workers kept the beds supplied with clean sheets, but patients often had to sleep two or three to a bed.

The Hôtel-Dieu was also a teaching hospital for medical students at the universities. The doctors-in-training examined patients to diagnose their illnesses. To treat the patients, they used techniques ranging from the practical to the supernatural. Doctors and students extracted teeth, set broken bones, and removed cataracts. They also consulted the stars, fed patients herbal mixes, and evaluated "humors," or fluids, that many medieval Parisians believed governed human personalities and health.

In the battle of 1346 (part of the Hundred Years' War), nine thousand English soldiers led by King Edward III defeated thirty thousand French soldiers *(above)*. A physician lances a patient's sore caused by the bubonic plague *(opposite)*. Although lancing was believed to encourage healing, the practice actually spread the disease.

War and Plague

In the mid-fourteenth century, a series of events turned Paris into a city of plague, war, violence, and famine for ninety-nine years. In 1346 King Edward III of England led an army into France. He hoped to gain the French crown and was supported by some families of French nobles. The armies ravaged the countryside, setting fire to fields and farms. In Paris the king raised taxes again and again to pay his troops. Angry mobs surged through the streets, hunting down tax collectors and government officials and destroying records.

An epidemic of the bubonic plague spread across Europe in the 1300s. The disease reached Paris in 1348. The disease, carried from rats to humans by fleas, was terribly contagious and almost always fatal. Many people handled dead bodies and became infected themselves. Some were left alone to die. In Paris the plague lasted for two years. By the time it was over, some fifty thousand people—half of the city's population—had died. And still France was at war.

In 1420 the English forces and their French allies captured Paris. Many of the remaining Parisians fled to begin new lives, far away from the war. Paris was almost deserted. Grass grew in the streets. Wolves roamed outside its walls, forcing people inside. People starved. When the city was freed by King Charles VII in 1436, many Parisians had been within the city walls for sixteen years. What became known as the Hundred Years' War was finally over. The later 1400s and the 1500s were a time of growth in Paris and throughout Europe. The city's population exploded, and *faubourgs* (suburbs) quickly sprang up outside the city walls. But daily life remained much the same as it had been for hundreds of years.

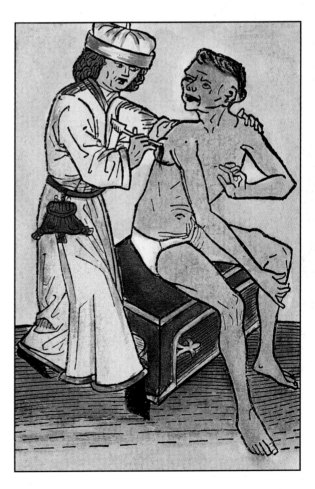

The Reformation

The Renaissance began in the 1400s. During this new age, artists and thinkers turned to the ideas of ancient Greece and Rome. People began thinking about their world in new ways. Arts and learning flourished, as did international trade. Europeans began to explore the globe. The printing press was invented. It made books cheaper and available to more people.

This was also a time of religious turmoil. In the early 1500s, some Christians in Germany separated from the Catholic Church to start a new Protestant Church. The movement, known as the Protestant Reformation, spread rapidly across Europe. The printing press played a role in the change. Both Catholics and Huguenots (a group of French Protestants) used it to create posters, books, and pamphlets advertising their views.

Some clashes between the groups were violent, such as the 1534 Affair of the Placards. Overnight, some people hung anti-Catholic posters across Paris. Although the posting had been the work of only a few people, French Catholics responded with panic. Suspects were arrested, and six were burned at the stake.

The government cracked down on people they called Protestant heretics. Protestant books were banned, and the government exiled or executed many Huguenots. Over the next fifty years, religious wars broke out across the country. Huguenot forces blockaded Paris for a short time in 1567, but hungry mobs poured out of the city to defeat them.

In 1572 many prominent Huguenots arrived in Paris to celebrate the marriage of the king's sister, a Catholic, to Henry of Navarre, a Protestant. All across Paris, people whispered rumors that the Huguenots planned to overthrow the king.

The king's mother, Catherine de Médicis, launched the St. Bartholomew's Day Massacre, which claimed three thousand Protestants in Paris and later eight thousand more in the rest of France. Catholic mobs and the royal militia killed men, women, and children. In 1589 Henry of Navarre became King Henry IV. When Catholic Parisians kept him out of the city, his forces attacked. Although nearly starving, the Parisians held firm. In 1594 King Henry IV converted to Catholicism and entered Paris. Tensions cooled when he issued the Edict of Nantes, which granted freedom of worship and civil rights to the Huguenots.

In this painting of the St. Bartholomew's Day Massacre, Huguenots are killed by members of the Catholic League.

The Enlightenment

At Paris salons, visitors discussed the ideas of French thinkers known as *philosophes*. The philosophes believed that, with careful thought, people could understand the world around them. They believed that, with a good education, each person could learn to make sensible life choices. They wanted to spread knowledge to everyone, and they also wanted to learn as much about the world as they could. The philosophes valued order and self-control, and they also believed in equal rights.

Salons, Theaters, and Promenades

King Henry IV worked hard to restore war-torn Paris. He restored royal dwellings, such as the Louvre, and ordered workers to pave more streets. Aristocrats and the rich built large, elaborate mansions called *hôtels* set within beautiful gardens. By the seventeenth century, factories that supplied the rich with tapestries, mirrors, glasswork, and other sumptuous furnishings were thriving in Paris. Wider streets, such as the Champs-Élysées, made it easier to travel in horse-drawn carriages. At the start of the 1600s, only a few rich people traveled in them, but one hundred years later, about twenty thousand carriages traveled the streets.

The rich of Paris had plenty of time to enjoy themselves. Young men learned how to ride horses and how to fence. Many rich people built tennis courts near their homes in the city. Some people gathered in private homes to eat, gossip, play cards, and argue. Called *salons*, these meetings attracted writers, philosophers, poets, magistrates, financiers, and members of the aristocracy. French drama flourished under the patronage of the rich. The rich perched in sumptuous boxes at the theaters, which allowed them to show off their splendid and elaborate costumes. The poor crowded into the pit in front of the stage.

All Parisians, rich and poor alike, enjoyed *la promenade* (walking). Men and women strolled the public parks and gardens, where they showed off new outfits or met friends. Aristocrats and the bourgeoisie mingled near the Palais-Royal, a building surrounded by lavish gardens, shops, theaters, and cafés. Lanterns cast a warm glow over the gardens in the evenings. The poor of Paris attended public dances, chatted with friends at taverns and cafés, and enjoyed public festivals with spectacular fireworks displays. But they worked long hours and had little time for fun.

A Hard Life

The gap between rich and poor widened during the seventeenth and eighteenth centuries. The middle class was made up of doctors, lawyers, writers, printers, architects, and painters. Although not rich, people of the middle class were well educated and lived in comfortable homes or apartments.

Most Parisians were very poor. The poor lived in the center of Paris, where ancient, patched-together houses lined twisting and turning streets. Advertisers slapped bills and posters onto the sides of houses. Gutters ran down the middle of the streets, which were covered with mud and garbage. When rain flooded the streets, people had to lay planks across the surging waters. At night the poorly lighted maze of streets became dangerous, and at times passersby were robbed or even murdered. Narrow alleys connected the streets to dark courtyards enclosed by more houses. Shops, cafés, and taverns occupied the ground floor of most

buildings. Inside the four or five stories above, families packed into tiny apartments.

By day the streets were crowded with vendors and tradespeople noisily peddling their wares. Each had a different cry; all yelled to make themselves heard. A vendor usually sold only one product, such as herring, coffee, fruit, or potatoes. Some were apprentices who had to spend their days selling instead of learning their trade. Others were skilled workers who offered to repair buckets, pans, or shoes.

In shops and small businesses, people worked hard all day long but made very little money. In the 1780s, bad harvests were followed by shortages of bread. People were hungry and blamed the rich, who had more than enough to eat.

In seventeenth- and eighteenth-century Paris, the poor *(opposite)* survived on a diet of bread and cheese, some fish, and almost no meat or vegetables. Baptisms *(above)* offered the poor a rare opportunity for celebration.

It was hard to get a steady supply of fresh water in Paris. Many people got their water right from the Seine or from public wells that dotted the city. Those who could afford it hired water carriers, who walked through the streets with buckets dangling from yokes on their shoulders.

The poor workers of Paris also paid high taxes. Over the past two hundred years, many people had left rural France looking for a better life in the big city. But most ended up begging on the street.

Liberté, Égalité, Fraternité!

On July 14, 1789, a mob of poor Parisians stormed the Bastille, an ancient fortresslike prison in the city. They hoped to free scores of political prisoners but found only seven people inside. Even so, the fall of the Bastille did accomplish something. It marked the beginning of the French Revolution, an event that shook Paris.

At that time, France was partially governed by a council. Called the États Généraux, it consisted of representatives of three groups—the aristocrats (the first estate), the Church (the second estate), and property-owning members of the bourgeoisie (the third estate). The very poor workers, who made up most of the population of Paris and who did not own any land, were outside of the system.

Many members of the third estate shared the Enlightenment ideals of the philosophes and believed that everyone should have a say in the government. In June 1789, the third estate renamed itself the National Assembly. That autumn the assembly passed the Declaration of the Rights of Man, which urged the formation of a new regime based on the Enlightenment ideals of liberty, equality, and pursuit of the common good.

The next five years were violent and bloody. Thousands of men and women were thrown into prison for holding counterrevolutionary beliefs. In September 1792, more than one thousand people were massacred when armed bands of revolutionaries broke into the prisons. On September 21, 1792, the revolutionaries declared the nation the French Republic.

Other European countries sent forces to Paris to suppress the Revolution but were beaten back. The next year, King Louis XVI and Queen Marie-Antoinette were imprisoned, tried, and beheaded at the guillotine.

Different revolutionary groups battled for control of the republic. Headed by a lawyer named Robespierre, a group called the Jacobins tried to maintain order. The Jacobins tried to end all dissent. Their efforts soon became known as the Reign of Terror. During the Reign of Terror, revolutionaries executed several thousand Parisians suspected of being enemies of the new regime. The Reign of Terror ended when Robespierre himself was guillotined. A more moderate revolutionary faction (group) then took power. They worked to bring stability back to Paris and to the rest of France.

The motto of France, *Liberté, Égalité, Fraternité*, dates from the French Revolution. The three ideals of Enlightenment thinkers—liberty, equality, and unity (or brotherhood)—were three main revolutionary goals.

Parisian peasants succeed in taking the Bastille *(above)*. The guillotine *(left)*, named for its inventor, the French physician Joseph Ignace Guillotin, made executions by the revolutionaries more efficient than ever.

During his ten-year reign, Napoléon I built new streets and monuments, including the Arc de Triomphe (which he never finished), and restored and expanded the Louvre. He is shown at his coronation *(above)* in 1804 and leading troops across the Alps *(right)*.

The Church in postrevolutionary France faced enormous changes. The government banned religious observances. Clerics were forced to renounce their vows. Churches that weren't torn down were stripped of their ornaments and statues. Many were used for nonreligious purposes, including the Cathedral of Notre Dame. Renamed the Temple of Reason, it became a place to hold meetings and performances. The Louvre, a royal palace, became a museum.

The Culture of Reason

The Revolution had overthrown the monarchy, but the poor and working-class people in Paris did not become more prosperous. The effects of the Revolution were felt in other ways. Revolutionary leaders, for example, instituted a new calendar. They considered the old calendar to be linked to religion, which the Revolution was against. Months were given names to match the seasons. Mars (March) was given the name Ventôse, or windy. Juillet (July) became Thermidor, or hot, and Janvier (January) was Pluviôs, or rainy. Years were counted from September 21, 1792, the day the French Republic was

declared. The date March 14, 1794, became 24 Ventôse, year II. But this new idea didn't stick. In 1806 the French government switched back.

The Revolution did not solve the bread shortage, and lines formed at bakeries long before the stores opened. Thousands of people died during the cold winters of the 1790s. Many beautiful hotels were deserted, and theaters, which could only show censored plays, closed early.

After the Revolution, France lurched through a series of governments. In 1799 a young army officer named Napoléon Bonaparte seized power. Within five years, he had proclaimed himself emperor of France. He gathered an army, which swiftly conquered parts of Italy and Prussia (modern-day Germany and Austria), but his assault on Russia was his undoing. When he tried to capture Moscow in 1813, the harsh Russian winter killed most of his soldiers. His empire began to crumble, and Prussian forces captured Paris with almost no struggle in 1814, forcing Napoléon's surrender.

As a result, he was exiled to the Mediterranean island of Elba. He escaped in 1815, rallied an enormous army, and arrived in France only to be defeated at the Battle of Waterloo. Exiled again, Napoléon died in 1821.

Beginning in 1850, more than twenty thousand buildings in Paris were torn down, with some neighborhoods completely razed. People who lived in the crumbling buildings had to move to other parts of the city or to the suburbs. About forty thousand new buildings were constructed.

CARBONNET

Rebuilding Paris

After Napoléon's defeat, France became a monarchy once more. But this time, France was also governed by the Chamber of Deputies, an elected body. Even so, two more revolutions shook France. When a king took away the right to vote, Parisians rioted until he resigned in the revolution of 1830. The new king, Louis-Philippe, ruled until 1848. During this time, railroads began to link Paris to other parts of France, and more factories were built in the city. Parisians were angry about poor economic conditions and corrupt government officials. In 1848 fighting again erupted in the streets of Paris. Mobs barricaded the winding streets for protection from soldiers who tried to quash the rebellions. Louis-Philippe fled his throne and Paris. After the revolution of 1848, Napoléon's nephew Louis-Napoléon was elected president. When his term was up, he proclaimed himself Emperor Napoléon III.

Napoléon III had grand plans for the city, which in 1850 had a population of one million. He appointed Georges-Eugène Haussmann, an urban planner, to change the face of the city. Many of the new structures were built in Second Empire style— five- and six-story apartment buildings with wide facades, mansard roofs, wrought iron balconies, and tall windows.

The Place du Parvis in front of Notre Dame was enlarged, and twelve boulevards were created to radiate from the Arc de Triomphe. The broad, tree-lined boulevards connected different sections of the city and allowed for a better flow of traffic. Fresh water was piped from springs and rivers outside the city. An improved system no longer poured sewage into the Seine.

Many criticized Haussmann's efforts, saying he cut the soul out of the city, destroyed historical structures, and drove out the working class. Others believed the changes were long overdue. In any case, Paris was a city transformed.

City of Painters

During and after the rebuilding of the city, there was a surge of activity among artists, writers, and musicians. One group of artists, the Impressionist painters, left a vivid record of Paris and its citizens. At first the painters' work wasn't well received by the art establishment in Paris. Impressionism seemed strange and unappealing. Instead of sticking to still-life scenes or landscape paintings like most artists of the time, the Impressionists painted scenes of people working, strolling, dancing, and eating. Rather than concentrating on fine details, the Impressionists were interested in exploring the effects of light, color, and movement.

The group included painters such as Claude Monet, Pierre-Auguste Renoir, Edgar Degas, Berthe Morisot, and Édouard Manet. They lived and worked in Montmartre, where many writers also had studios. Many of their paintings and drawings capture the lively street life of this section of town, including the cafés, dance halls, and artists' studios. Both Renoir and Monet painted the bustling Pont Neuf, the city's oldest bridge. Monet obtained permission to paint inside the Louvre, but instead of copying the masterpieces that were hung on the walls, as most aspiring artists did, he painted the city from the second-story balconies.

It took some time before the paintings could be recognized both for their artistic merit and as skillful impressions of a shiny, newly rebuilt city. In modern times, Impressionist paintings hang in museums all around the world.

The paintings of artists Édouard Manet *(painting shown in inset)* and Camille Pissarro *(shown left)* rocked the Paris art world.

The Big Stores

As Paris acquired its new look, an innovation in the city would change the face of cities everywhere—the *grand magasin,* or department store. Instead of small, specialized stores, the grand magasins offered an enormous selection of products, all under one roof. Shoppers didn't have to bargain with merchants anymore, because low prices were clearly marked on each piece of merchandise.

The first to open, Au Bon Marché, had a magnificent staircase connecting the floors and a glass roof over shoppers' heads. Thanks to advances in building technology, large street-level windows allowed sellers to create inviting displays. What made the stores most inviting, though, was the sheer volume of goods to browse through.

French novelist Émile Zola wrote *Au Bonheur des Dames (The Ladies' Paradise)*, a fictional account of one such store. In it he describes his heroine's experience when she visits the store for the first time:

"There she saw, in the open street, on the very pavement, a mountain of cheap goods—bargains, placed there to tempt the passersby and attract attention. Hanging from above were pieces of woolen and cloth goods, merinos, cheviots, and tweeds, floating like flags; the neutral, slate, navy-blue, and olive-green tints being relieved by the large white price-tickets. Close by, round the doorway, were hanging strips of fur, narrow bands for dress trimmings, fine Siberian squirrel-skin, spotless snowy swansdown, rabbit-skin imitation ermine, and imitation sable. Below, on shelves and on tables, amidst a pile of remnants, appeared an immense quantity of hosiery almost given away; knitted woolen gloves, neckerchiefs, women's hoods, waistcoats, a winter show in all colors, striped, dyed, and variegated, with here and there a flaming patch of red…. There seemed to be an immense clearance sale going on; the establishment seemed bursting with goods, blocking up the pavement with surplus."

Paris's new department stores, such as La Ville de Saint-Denis *(above)*,
made shopping an exciting experience. Ads attracted shoppers by boasting
of the value of the stores' goods *(left inset)*.

Paris Is Blockaded

Paris's beautiful new boulevards and gleaming buildings could not prepare the city for the trial that it would face in the early 1870s. France went to war with Prussia in 1870. After a mere six weeks, the enemy captured the French emperor. Back in Paris, a group of deputies took the opportunity to proclaim the end of the empire and the beginning of a republic.

The French army weakened, and the Prussians surrounded Paris. Parisians faced a hard winter under siege. Food was scarce, and fresh vegetables, milk, and meat became impossible to obtain, except through the black market. Parisians butchered horses and pigeons. Zoo animals, including two prized elephants, were killed for food.

Parisians used the hot-air balloon to

Prussians fire on a French balloon in the Franco-Prussian War *(above)*, while Parisians continue to manufacture more balloons in a Paris factory *(right)*.

communicate with the outside world. The balloons had been invented almost one hundred years before. When the siege began, citizens began to send letters and documents with aeronauts, who flew the balloons over the enemy and out into the countryside. During the siege, eleven tons of dispatches flew out of the city. Of the sixty-five balloons that the Parisians launched, only five fell into enemy hands.

France signed a peace treaty with Prussia in February 1871, ending the blockade. The conservative elected body, called the Assembly, was unpopular. A rival government, the Commune, took charge of the city. For ten weeks, the government troops and the Communards fought in the streets. The Communards were defeated in a bloody fight at a cemetery on the edge of Paris.

In the late 1800s, middle- and working-class people found they had more leisure time and more money in their pockets. Paris provided many ways to spend both. The carnival atmosphere that settled on the city gave the era its nickname, the Belle Époque, meaning the "beautiful era."

The Belle Époque

The bloodshed and unrest of the past hundred years ended for the last decades of the nineteenth century. An improved sewer system and gas and electrical power made life more comfortable for the middle and working classes. For the first time, the government established public schools for children to attend. Mass production and better transportation meant that day-to-day necessities were cheaper and easier to buy. Useful, labor-saving devices such as bicycles and sewing machines made life easier. Electric streetlights lit the streets after dark, an improvement that made it safer and easier to travel through Paris at night.

Music halls let audiences eat and drink as they watched jugglers, clowns, and musicians perform. The dancers at one hall, called the Moulin Rouge, created a daring new dance called the cancan. Cafés were crowded with Parisians enjoying coffee, beer, and wine. Families flocked to circuses and fairs.

Paris was eager to show off its spruced-up streets. The city hosted three world's fairs in twenty years. Tourists came to town to ride on roller coasters, visit exhibits of new technology, or look at a replica of the Bastille. An especially popular attraction was built for the 1889 Exposition—the thousand-foot-tall Eiffel Tower, then the tallest structure in the world. Visitors climbed steps to the top or took elevators to enjoy the forty-mile view.

A new art form combined modern technology with entertainment. In 1895 Louis-Jean Lumière gave the first showing of films that showed moving images. The movies soon became wildly popular. And in 1900, the Paris subway system, the Métro, opened with ten three-car trains.

Upper-class Parisians enjoy a masked ball at a Paris theater (opposite). Laborers work on the construction of the Eiffel Tower in October 1888 (above).

World War I and After

In 1914 World War I spread across Europe. France joined Great Britain and Russia in fighting Germany and the Austro-Hungarian Empire. At the beginning of the war, the German army came dangerously close to Paris—only twenty-five miles away at the Marne River. But the French held the line. When they needed reinforcements, French general Joseph-Simon Gallieni requisitioned Paris taxicabs to help transport troops to the front. More than two thousand cabs carried soldiers to the front lines. The troops pushed back the German army. The victory became known as the "Miracle of the Marne."

The fighting didn't threaten the city for another three and a half years, but Parisians felt the effects of the war all the same. Fuel and food were rationed, and morale wore thin as years of fighting continued. In 1918 Germans shelled the city with Big Bertha, a giant long-range gun that damaged some buildings and killed about two hundred people. But the German army never entered the city. The leaders of the warring nations signed an armistice later that year.

The treaty that set peace terms was signed at Versailles, outside of Paris, in 1919. The signing was followed by a full military parade down the Champs-Élysées.

After the war, Paris again attracted artists from all across Europe and even North America. Painter Pablo Picasso, filmmaker Jean Cocteau, and composer Erik Satie opened studios and set to work. The city also lured Americans, many of whom had visited Paris as soldiers. They returned, drawn by the low cost of living and the abundance of other artists. Writers and artists such as Ernest Hemingway, Man Ray, Gertrude Stein, and Berenice Abbott not only took their inspiration from the city's creative atmosphere, but often worked the city into their art as well.

> *There is never any ending to Paris….Paris was always worth it and you received return for whatever you brought to it.*
> —Ernest Hemingway,
> *A Moveable Feast*

People gather around the Arc de Triomphe to celebrate peace in 1919 *(right)*.

Nazis Occupy Paris

During World War II (1939–1945), Paris suffered greatly. In 1939 Germany's Nazi army thundered through Belgium. Some Parisians braced themselves for an invasion. Others loaded their possessions onto cars, bicycles, and carts and fled south. By June three hundred thousand people left the city each day. On June 14, 1940, the German army marched down the Champs-Élysées and hung a Nazi swastika at the Hôtel de Ville,

the city hall. A week later, the German leader Adolf Hitler came to survey his conquest. His visit included a stop at Napoléon's tomb.

For the next four years, Nazi soldiers occupied the city. Rationing made it difficult for Parisians to get fuel. Food rationing left Parisians malnourished. Private cars were banned. Newspapers were censored. Nazi soldiers bullied residents and persecuted Jewish Parisians—many of whom were sent to concentration camps.

Many Parisians cooperated with the Nazis and tried to live as usual. Some Parisians joined the Résistance, which tried to undermine the Nazis with pamphlets, radio broadcasts, and sabotage. The efforts often led to more repression.

In August 1944, the Allies (the anti-German international alliance) approached Paris. The Parisians rose up against the Nazis. The people of Paris barricaded the streets and attacked with everything from homemade explosives to rocks to guns. Soon after the Allies arrived on August 24, the Nazis were driven from Paris. The Résistance leader, General Charles de Gaulle, led a triumphant march down the Champs-Élysées.

German troops roll into Paris along the Champs-Élysées
in June 1940 *(left)*. Nazi officers at a French café
(above) command attention from passersby.

After the War

aris faced the difficult task of putting itself back together after the war ended. Bridges, factories, and railroads that had been destroyed in the war needed to be rebuilt. The political situation was unstable, with government leaders changing several times a year. General de Gaulle formed an emergency government in 1958. Under his direction, France approved a new constitution, and de Gaulle was elected president.

Paris was becoming a more modern city. Cars filled the streets. Workers widened and resurfaced roads. The Métro and bus systems were improved. Builders and planners debated whether skyscrapers should be built among the city's historical buildings. They compromised by agreeing that skyscrapers could be built only on the fringes of the city. Les Halles, the open-air market that had been in existence for centuries, was torn down. In its place went a shopping center and Le Centre Pompidou, a glass-walled art museum.

The city received a big jolt in May 1968. University students began a series of strikes. They were unhappy with crowded classrooms and other university problems. Many disagreed with the de Gaulle government and the war in Vietnam (a former French colony). The strikes spread from campuses to the general working population, where people were frustrated by economic conditions. Workers all across France went on strike, bringing production and transportation to a standstill for a month.

A Love of Fine Food

Paris has long been known as a capital of fine food and dining. The streets are lined with bakeries, the windows piled with flaky croissants, crusty baguettes, and buttery *pain au chocolat* (chocolate croissants). Cheese shops are packed with pungent blue cheese and tangy goat cheese. Chocolate shops offer beautifully made bonbons and candied chestnuts.

The love of good food makes dining out an important part of Parisian life. The city has famous gourmet restaurants where a splendid, many-course meal can last for hours. But Parisians also meet their friends at neighborhood restaurants—homey bistros where dinner can be a hearty plate of beef stew or roasted chicken.

Paris's fame as a city of restaurants began after the French Revolution. Skilled chefs had traditionally prepared delicious meals for the city's nobility. But most nobles had been executed or fled the country during the Reign of Terror. So chefs opened restaurants, where they

served elaborate meals to anyone who could pay for them. The fame of the city's restaurants spread all across the globe.

Many Parisians prepare delicious meals at home, too. They buy their ingredients from small shops close to home or visit one of the many large outdoor markets of Paris, where they can pick from piles of colorful vegetables or select freshly caught fish.

The tables are always well provided; the Parisians never eat alone, they like to sip rather than drink, but then they sip often, and always ask their guests to do the same....There is not a population in the world more industrious or so badly off, because they spend all their money on their stomach and their [clothes]....
—Charles Cotolendi, an eighteenth-century lawyer

It is hard to walk Paris's streets without being tempted by the lure of pastries, fresh fish, and piles of colorful fruits and vegetables.

The Métro

The Métro, short for the French terms for "metropolitan railroad," has been an important part of Paris since 1900. When the subway opened, elaborate Art Nouveau wrought ironwork framed its entrances. Some of those entrances still stand, but most stations have modern entrances with escalators and automatic turnstiles.

Parisians heading to work, school, or home ride the Métro. The trains wind their way along 124 miles of track above and below the city streets, linking 368 stations. In fact, no point in Paris is more than five hundred yards from a station. Color-coded maps help riders plot their routes and transfer from one line to another.

Métro stations bustle with activity. Advertising posters line the walls, street musicians perform in the passages between tracks, and announcements occasionally blare from loudspeakers. The names of some of the stops are spelled out in intricate mosaic lettering, and other stops feature displays reflecting their location.

The Métro, a lifeline for city residents, carries some 6 million people a day.

The Métro in Paris carries millions of people a day on 3,500 cars. During World War II, people used the Métro stations as bomb shelters during raids. The stations also offered warm places to spend time when people ran out of heating fuel.

Parisians love to walk. And no wonder! Expanded boulevards offer hundreds of cafés, sidewalk vendors, and entrances to stores selling everything from the latest clothing fashions to souvenirs, music, and freshly cut flowers.

A City for Walking

The Métro helps Parisians get where they need to go quickly and allows them to travel long distances. But the best way to see Paris is on foot. For active, noisy street life, the wide boulevards offer crowded sidewalks and big stores selling everything from compact discs to stylish shoes. Take a break at one of the sidewalk cafés and order a sandwich, a soda, or a pastry. Chairs right on the sidewalks guarantee a view of the passing crowds.

Street vendors sell handicrafts and wind-up birds. Drummers and guitar players keep a steady beat for passersby. Paris has many quiet back streets, where you'll see beautiful old apartment buildings, cozy restaurants, and little shops. Tiny, ancient streets only a few feet wide remind Parisians of how the city looked in the Middle Ages.

Paris also has many parks for walkers, from small neighborhood squares to larger, more elegant spaces. Strollers amble through the little neighborhood parks, while children clamber over jungle gyms. Parents push strollers, grandparents feed birds from park benches, and schoolchildren sail boats in fountains. People play basketball at the lovely Jardin du Luxembourg or sketch the statues of the Jardin des Tuileries.

The Bois de Boulogne is a big woods at the edge of town, where people can go to the horse races, visit an amusement park, or simply stroll down a tree-lined path.

The Sacré-Coeur church tower rises up above the romantic nightlife of Paris.

Modern-Day Paris

Paris is a vibrant, cosmopolitan city that attracts millions of businesspeople and tourists from all over the world. Over the years, the city has added modern touches to its centuries-old splendor. For example, the Louvre sports a glass pyramid in its courtyard, and the modern complex La Défense includes a contemporary version of the Arc de Triomphe. These days, more than 2 million people live in the city and its suburbs. The twenty *arrondissements* (quarters) that make up Paris create a city of distinct neighborhoods. Some are home to thousands of immigrants from Asia, Africa, and eastern Europe. Some house people whose families have lived in Paris for generations.

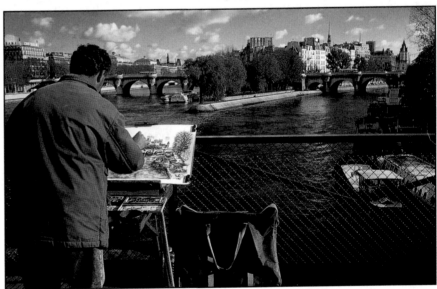

(Left) Paris's famed Arc de Triomphe rises above the flood of night traffic. (Top, clockwise from left) Common Paris scenes include friends gathering at outdoor cafés, colorful shops, and artists mastering the city's abundant riverscapes.

Paris believes in honoring its past. In 1989 Paris was at the center of fantastic celebrations commemorating the two-hundredth anniversary of the republic with fireworks, parades, and festivities. An old railroad station has been converted into a museum displaying the works of the Impressionist painters. Parisians attend mass at Notre Dame and leave the Île de la Cité by walking over the Pont Neuf, built in 1607. All across the globe, the name Paris conjures up thoughts of delicious food, wonderful art, beautiful fashions, and historic landmarks.

Paris Timeline

	First Millennium B.C.	First and Second Millennium A.D.
300 B.C.–A.D. 1000 **Early History**	**THIRD CENTURY B.C.** **53 B.C.**	Parisians settle on Île de la Cité Roman army, led by Julius Caesar, arrives
	FIRST CENTURY A.D. **THIRD CENTURY A.D.**	Romans build town of Lutetia Saint Denis arrives to establish Christianity and is beheaded
A.D. 500–1572 **Middle Ages**	**A.D. 885** **A.D. 987** **A.D. 1163** **A.D. 1200** **A.D. 1348** **A.D. 1420–1436**	Vikings raid Paris for seventh and final time Hugh Capet becomes king of France; Paris is made the capital Construction begins on Notre Dame Cathedral University of Paris founded Bubonic plague strikes France Paris under English rule
A.D. 1572–1804 **Renaissance and** **Revolution**	**A.D. 1572** **A.D. 1600s** **A.D. 1774** **A.D. 1789** **A.D. 1793–1794** **A.D. 1799**	St. Bartholomew's Day Massacre Palace of Versailles built Louis XVI ascends to throne Mob captures Bastille; French Revolution begins Reign of Terror; Louis XVI and Queen Marie-Antoinette executed Napoléon Bonaparte seizes power

Second Millennium A.D.

A.D. 1804–1914 Age of Reason		
	A.D. **1804**	Napoléon crowns himself emperor
	A.D. **1815**	Napoléon defeated at Waterloo
	A.D. **1830**	Three-day revolution forces abdication of King Charles X; Louis-Philippe becomes king
	A.D. **1848**	Revolution of 1848; Napoléon III (Louis-Napoléon) takes power
	A.D. **1855**	Baron Georges-Eugène Haussmann begins major reconstruction of Paris
	A.D. **1870–71**	Franco-Prussian War; Paris under siege by Prussian army; Napoléon III abdicates; establishment of the Paris Commune
	A.D. **1889**	The Eiffel Tower is built

A.D. 1914– Modern Paris		
	A.D. **1914**	France enters World War I; Battle of the Marne fought 25 miles from Paris
	A.D. **1918**	Armistice signed; World War I ends
	A.D. **1939**	France enters war with Germany
	A.D. **1940**	Paris occupied by Nazis
	A.D. **1944**	Paris liberated
	A.D. **1945**	World War II ends
	A.D. **1958**	Charles de Gaulle elected president
	A.D. **1968**	Students and workers strike across France
	A.D. **1969**	Charles de Gaulle resigns
	A.D. **1989**	France celebrates two-hundredth anniversary of republic
	A.D. **2000**	Eiffel Tower is scene of grand fireworks display

Books about France and Paris

Aaseng, Nathan. *Paris*. New York: New Discovery Books, 1992.

Aliki. *The King's Day: Louis XIV of France*. New York: Thomas Y. Crowell, 1989.

Besson, Jean-Louis, and Carol Volk, trans. *October 45: Childhood Memories of the War*. Mankato, MN: Creative Editions, 1995.

France in Pictures. Minneapolis: Lerner Publications Company, 1998.

Ganeri, Anita, and Rachel Wright. *France*. New York: Franklin Watts, 1993.

Gilbert, Adrian. *The French Revolution*. New York: Thomson Learning, 1995.

Marrin, Albert. *Napoleon and the Napoleonic Wars*. New York: Viking, 1991.

Martell, Hazel Mary. *The Normans*. New York: New Discovery Books, 1992.

Munro, Roxie. *The Inside-Outside Book of Paris*. New York: Dutton Children's Books, 1992.

Pernoud, Régine. *A Day with a Noblewoman*. Minneapolis: Runestone Press, 1997.

Pflaum, Rosalynd. *Marie Curie and Her Daughter Irène*. Minneapolis: Lerner Publications Company, 1993.

Roberts, Jeremy. *Saint Joan of Arc*. Minneapolis: Lerner Publications Company, 2000.

Sookram, Brian. *France*. New York: Chelsea House, 1990.

Stein, R. Conrad. *Paris*. New York: Children's Press, 1996.

Waldee, Lynne Marie. *Cooking the French Way* (Easy Menu Ethnic Cookbooks). Minneapolis: Lerner Publications Company, 1982.

Zipes, Jack, trans. *Beauties, Beasts, and Enchantments: Classic French Fairy Tales*. New York: New American Library, 1989.

Index

About the Author and Illustrator

Sarah Hoban has had a lifelong interest in Paris and has visited the city often. A former magazine editor, she is now a full-time writer and editor, specializing in travel, food, and business-related subjects. This is her first children's book. She lives near Chicago, Illinois, with her baby daughter and her husband, who, coincidentally, grew up in Paris.

Bob Moulder of Derby, England, studied art in Belfast, Northern Ireland. He is a specialist in historical artwork and comic strips. He is an accomplished author of history books, and his artwork has appeared in leading publications in the United Kingdom. He currently works with the Oxford Illustrators and Designers group.

Acknowledgments

For quoted material: p. 40, Emile Zola. *Au Bonheur des Dames (The Ladies' Paradise)*. (Berkeley, CA: University of California Press, 1992); p. 47, Ernest Hemingway. *A Moveable Feast*. (New York: Collier Books, 1964); p. 53, Paul LaCroix. *France in the Eighteenth Century*. (New York: Frederick Ungar Publishing Co., 1963).

For photographs and art reproductions: p. 5 ©Jean-Marc Truchet/Tony Stone Images, Inc.; p. 6 ©Chad Ehlers/Tony Stone Images, Inc.; pp. 14–15, 19, 25, 33 (inset), 34 The Granger Collection; p. 20–21 North Wind Pictures; p. 24, 40–41, 43, 45 Mary Evans Picture Library; p. 27 ©Erich Lessing/Art Resource; p. 30–31, 35 (inset) Musée du Louvre, Paris/SuperStock; p. 33 Explorer, Paris/SuperStock; p. 38 Hermitage Museum, St. Petersburg, Russia/Superstock; p. 38 (inset) Musée des Beaux-Arts, Tournai, Belgium/Giraudon, Paris/Superstock; p. 42 Stock Montage, Inc.; p. 44 Christie's Images, London/Bridgeman Art Library, London/Superstock; p. 47 Christie's Images/Superstock; p. 48 Archive France/Archive Photos; p. 49 Corbis-UPI/Bettmann; p. 52–53, 54–55, 59 (right) ©Dave Toht; p. 56©Robert Frerck/Tony Stone Images, Inc.; p. 56 (inset) ©Tim Macpherson/Tony Stone Images, Inc.; p. 57 Chad Ehlers/Tony Stone Images, Inc.; p. 58 ©Ron Sanford/Tony Stone Images, Inc.; p. 59 (left) ©Bob Handelman/Tony Stone Images, Inc.; p. 59 (right) ©Bertrand Rieger/Tony Stone Images, Inc. Cover: Hermitage Museum, St. Petersburg, Russia/SuperStock.